Welcome to the Isle of Man, a little island nestled in the Irish Sea between Scotland and England to the east, Wales to the south and Ireland to the west.

Spend a full day in the magical, fairy kingdom of the Fairy Bridge. Discover how the tiny, mystical folk co-exist with all the nature around them.

What do they do all day?

Find out if all the human travellers over the Fairy Bridge will greet the fairies today. And what might the fairies do if anyone fails to hail them politely?

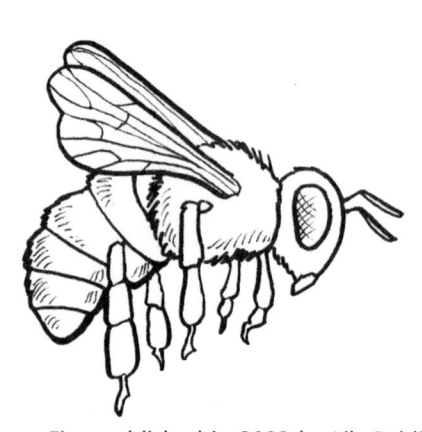

First published in 2023 by Lily Publications on behalf of the author.
All rights reserved. ©Anita Mulvey 2023.

The rights of Anita Mulvey to be identified as the author of this work and Julia Ashby Smyth as the illustrator have been asserted in accordance with section 77 of the Copyright, Designs and patents act 1988.

www.juliaashbysmyth.com

www.lilypublications.co.uk

ISBN 978-1-83808-459-2

Typeset in Malgun Gothic 14pt

Lily Publications

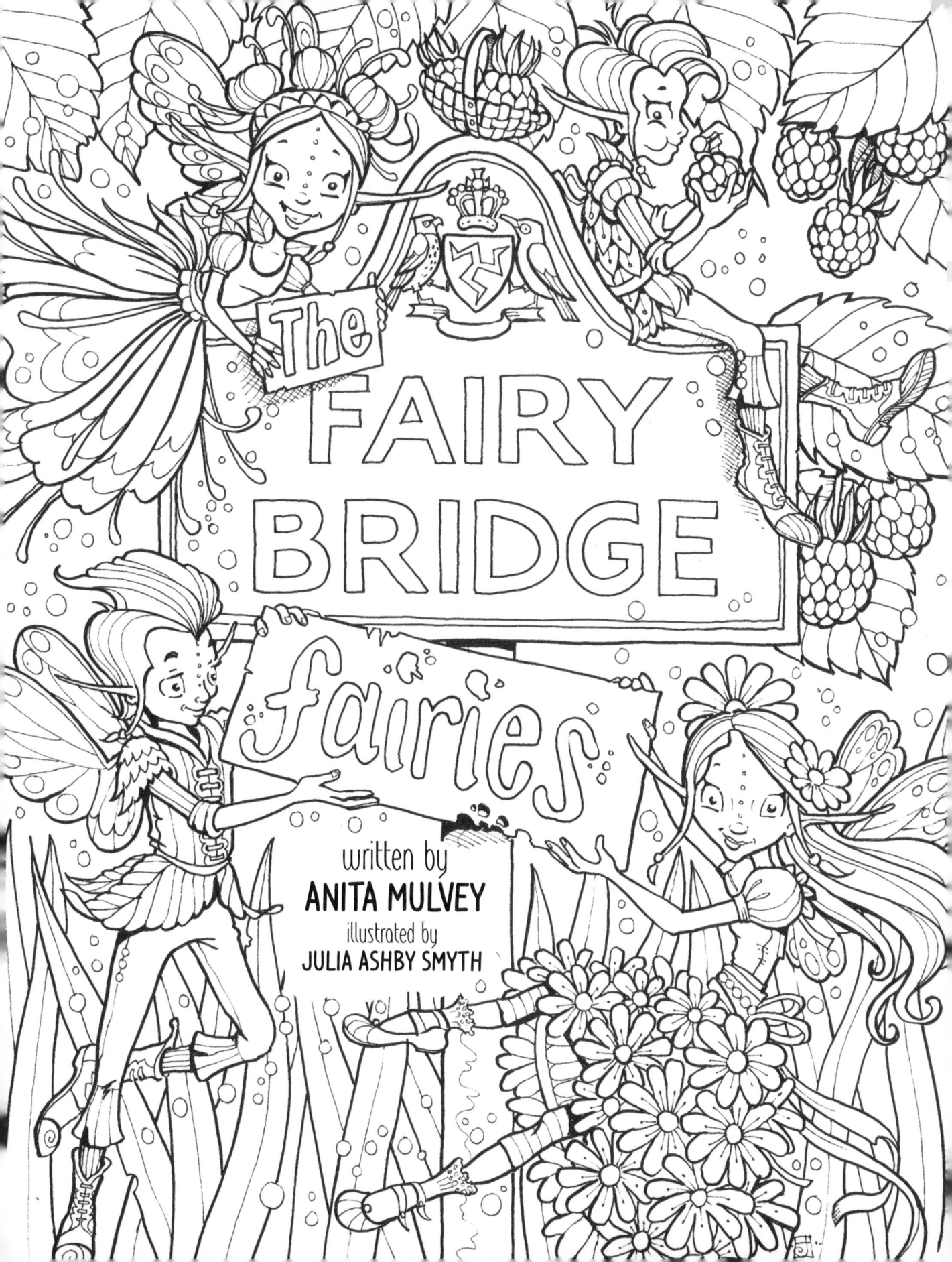

The FAIRY BRIDGE fairies

written by
ANITA MULVEY

illustrated by
JULIA ASHBY SMYTH

Chapter 1

Once upon a time, there was a little island in the middle of the Irish Sea. This island had a mountain called Mount Snaefell, which was named 'Snow Fell' mountain by Viking invaders long, long ago.

If you climb Mount Snaefell or take the tiny vintage train to the top, there is a fabulous view of the island, the sea surrounding it and distant lands. A sign declares that seven kingdoms can be seen from the viewpoint at the very top of the mountain: the kingdoms of England, Scotland, Wales, Ireland, Heaven, the Sea and Man. The last kingdom on this list is so named because the little island is the Isle of Man.

The ancient sea god Manannan gave the island its name. He can be quite capricious and often throws his cloak of mist right over his island. On these days, it can be difficult to see any of the kingdoms from the summit, Man included!

But what many people do not know is that there are actually eight kingdoms. The smallest and most secret is the Fairy Kingdom.

Oh yes, fairies do indeed exist; it's just that very few people ever get to see them!

Fairies are tiny, magical beings. They have wings, so they can fly wherever they wish. There might even be fairies living at the bottom of your garden and you just wouldn't know!

But the vast majority of the Isle of Man's fairies live in the south of the island. Yet, if you do want to see Manx fairies, you should head for the Fairy Bridge. However, even here they are very rarely seen.

Our story starts on a beautiful, sunny day in May. It is very early and the Fairy Bridge fairies are just beginning to stir. One by one, they open their eyes, yawn and stretch right down to their tiny toes. Each fairy gets dressed, either folding their little pyjamas neatly or putting them in the washing bag.

Then they find a sunny spot on the grassy bank by the stream and open out their miniature wings so that they can dry in the sun's warmth. Their wings are truly beautiful: delicate and translucent with symmetrical patterns of silvery veins threading through them.

Some fairies' wings have silky smooth edges whereas others have frilled edges which are perfectly natural but seem to have been created by the tiniest and prettiest pinking shears imaginable. As their wings become dry, the fairies give them a little flutter then gently fold them away.

Now the fairies can concentrate on breakfast. They each fill an acorn cup with dew collected from the leaves of their favourite flowers. Most fairies nibble on a blackberry, but some of them choose a raspberry or strawberry instead. The fairies are so small that they need both hands to hold their fruit and just one berry is enough to fill them up until lunchtime.

You might be thinking that these berries are not actually ready to pick and eat in May, but fairies are magical beings. They can find ripe fruit, vegetables, herbs, seeds and nuts growing around the Fairy Bridge whenever they want!

Each fairy then washes in water magically collected from the stream in little shells. Some fairies then use moss to dry themselves but many of the younger ones simply bask in the sunshine and dry off naturally.

It is very difficult to tell how old a fairy is. Don't forget that they are magical and rarely appear older or younger than each other. But you should never ask a fairy their age as this is the height of bad manners in fairy society!

All the fairies clean their teeth with toothbrushes carefully constructed out of friendly cats' whiskers tied onto tiny twigs. Once they have brushed their hair using brushes made from pine needles, they are ready for the day ahead. Everyone is practically sparkling!

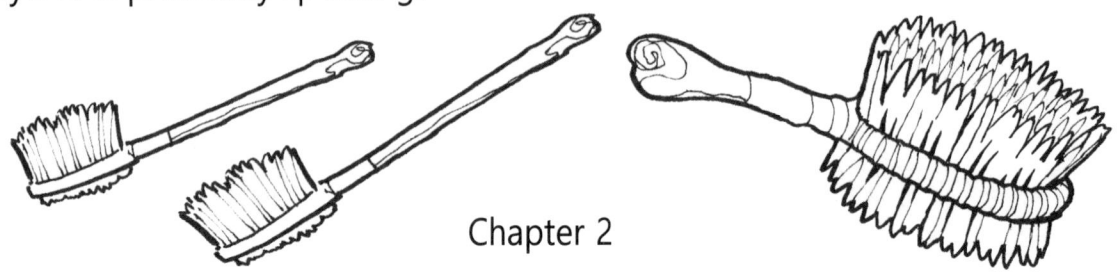

Chapter 2

Bramble flies up to the bridge's parapet with his best friends Alder and Spruce. As soon as they arrive to take up the morning guard duty, the three night guards yawn, stretch and get ready to go down for their breakfast and a nice long sleep. Chestnut and Hickory fly away immediately, leaving Elm to report that the night watch was trouble-free before he flies off as well.

Bramble and his best friends take up position to watch everything travelling south on the road. They are so little that just about all the humans passing by will fail to notice them. But anyone astute and lucky enough to see them would be impressed with their smart outfits in varying shades of green.

Each boy's top is decorated with a leaf or needle pattern corresponding to the plant or tree he is named after. So Bramble and Alder have leaves on their tops but Spruce has the needles of spruce trees to adorn his outfit

The twin girl fairies Flora and Fleur take up guard duty on the other side of the road. Bluebell flies up to join them and so the female night watchers can retire, sleepy but happy after an uneventful night. As Rose, Violet and Daisy fly away, their replacements are ready to watch everything travelling north.

They settle happily, smoothing out their colourful skirts which contrast well with their pale satin tops. Bluebell's skirt is like most of the other fairies' skirts, cleverly made to resemble the petals of the flower she is named after. The twins, however, have more unusual skirts patterned with multi-coloured flowers of all varieties.

A yellow car drives past the Fairy Bridge going north towards Douglas, the capital of the Isle of Man. Practically invisible, the girl fairies nod contentedly as the car driver mutters "Hello" to them on his way to work.

A cyclist rides by next, travelling just a short way south to a stable yard in Ballasalla where she works looking after horses. The fairies recognise her at once as she pedals to and fro every day.

Unbeknown to the young woman, she is quite a favourite with all the fairies as she never fails to say hello and always greets them in Manx.

As she rides past, the lady calls cheerfully, "Moghrey mie, Mooinjer Veggey!"("Good morning, Little People!" which is how all speakers of Manx Gaelic would address fairies).

All the fairies cheer and wish her a good morning too. The fairies accept all kinds of greetings and really don't mind which languages are used to hail them, but they definitely love Manx best!

Shortly after this, a black car drives south towards the airport at Ronaldsway. The driver is a young woman with her baby strapped in his child's seat in the Back.

"Morning, fairies," the driver cries as she crosses the bridge. "Say hello to the fairies, Peter," she tells her baby. He is too young to talk yet, but he gurgles and chuckles at her words.

The boy fairies are delighted and accept both responses as suitable greetings. Chuckling too, Alder gives a friendly wave to the baby although Peter doesn't notice, of course.

The next vehicle to cross the bridge is a bright red motorbike. The rider is travelling south to Castletown, the former capital of the island, to visit his grandmother. He nods his head graciously towards the fairy boys and chugs on his way. Unseen by the motorcyclist, the fairies nod in return.

The six fairies by the road continue their duty, sitting happily in the sunshine. Everyone passing them so far has greeted them in some way or other.

Would all the human travellers be as polite today?
And what might the fairies do if anyone fails to hail them?

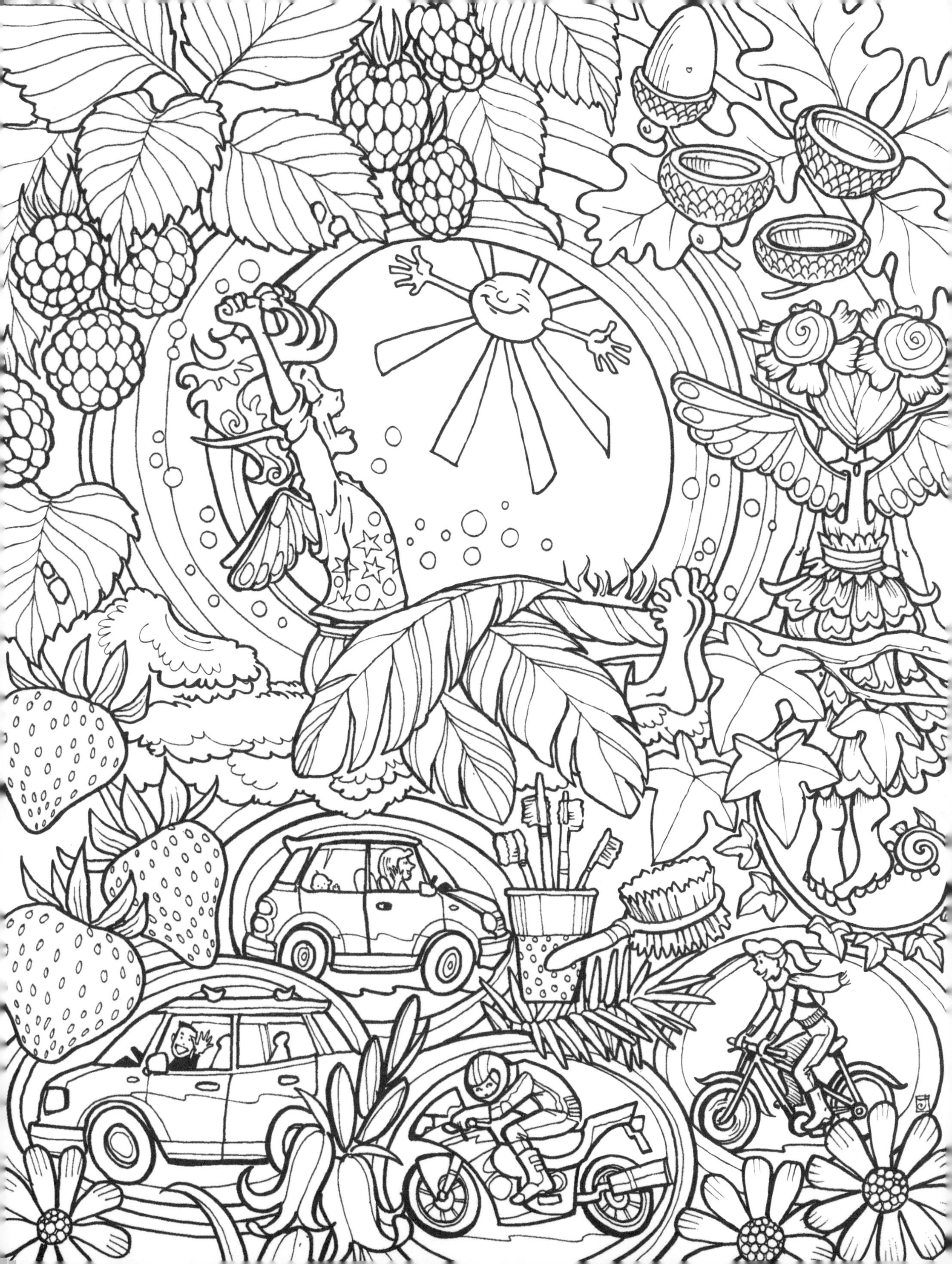

Chapter 3

Meanwhile, all their companions except the sleeping night guards, are busy below the bridge. Lilac and Freesia chop peppermint leaves so that they are the right size for their tiny teapot. Lily and Daffodil collect up the prepared leaves and store them in thimbles, carefully placing small, flat pebbles on top as lids.

When they have finished, they stack the full thimbles on the lowest brick jutting out slightly under the south side of their bridge.

Mistletoe, Ivy and Holly get to work grinding acorns which the fairies love as coffee. Though the boys are not real triplets or even related at all, they are such close friends that they seem to be identical brothers. They always do everything together and can only be distinguished by the different leaf patterns on their tops.

Cedar and Willow scoop up the ground acorns and pour them into eggcups with more little, flat pebbles for lids. Next they place the full eggcups on the second lowest brick jutting out under the south side of their bridge.

There is quite a crowd of fairies down by the stream. Barefoot and with lots of splashing and giggling, Hyacinth, Buddleia and Pansy are right in the shallowest water washing little fairy clothes. They pass each dripping item to Hazel and Ash who are waiting on the stream's bank to wring out as much water as they can before passing them on again.

Sycamore and Snowdrop, two of the youngest and most energetic fairies, spend the morning taking the washing to the bushes near the stream and pegginig it out to dry.

They have a collection of hedgehog prickles kept neatly in the lid of an old fountain pen. Skilfully the two young fairies bend and twist each prickle to hold the washing securely so that it won't blow away in the breeze.

Snowdrop and Sycamore start off by racing up and down the slope of the grassy bank. As the day progresses, they get slower and slower, so that they are trotting up and down by the middle of the morning and coffee time.

After resting with an acorn cup of tasty acorn coffee, they set off by jogging. But soon even their youthful fairy legs begin to tire, so of course they fly up and down. They race each other, flying for fun.

All the fairy washing is too minuscule to be seen by any passing humans. But if you could see it, you would smile at the sight of their colourful, little clothes pegged out on the bushes to dry. Even Sycamore and Snowdrop are giggling as they peg out the tiny undergarments!

Chapter 4

A small team of fairies set off for a gentle walk through the beautiful Manx countryside. They are having a relaxing morning before sleeping during the afternoon because they will be on duty on the bridge overnight. The Fairy Bridge fairies are a democratic lot, so everyone shares the jobs and takes fair turns at everything. Who knows, perhaps this is why they are called 'fairies'? In any event, the minute, magical beings actually enjoy all their 'tasks', so they are really sharing out the fun anyway!

As they stroll, they carry little baskets made out of the finest reeds found growing in the shallows of the stream. The reeds have been twisted together and the fairies are proud of the woven baskets which they store carefully in an old yogurt pot which they found and cleaned long ago.

They keep their container of miniature baskets handy on the third lowest brick jutting out under the south side of their bridge.

Juniper and Elder are the first fairies to see the bees. Of course, the insects seem absolutely enormous to the tiny fairies, but they are not afraid. All fairies are on the friendliest of terms with all the wildlife around them.

The bees spot the fairies and greet their friends with a happy buzz. They even manage to buzz a little quieter than normal so as not to hurt the delicate, little fairy ears!

The bees give the fairies some honey. Azalea wraps the precious sweet stuff in a maple leaf, carefully tucking in the three pointed edges so as not to lose even a drop. The fairies know that honey will keep perfectly well once stored like this in leaves on the fourth lowest brick jutting out under the south side of their Bridge.

The fairies spend a few minutes magically chatting with the friendly bees before continuing their leisurely ramble. They find some hazelnuts and collect just a couple of them in Rowan's basket. His small basket is now full and the nuts will easily feed all the fairies after they have been ground down. This will probably be on the rota for some of their fairy friends tomorrow.

The fairies are tiny, so they do not need many nuts or too many of any of nature's stores. So you can see that the fairies share all the produce fairly with all the other living creatures around them. After they have ambled on, a little mouse will eat his share of the nuts too.

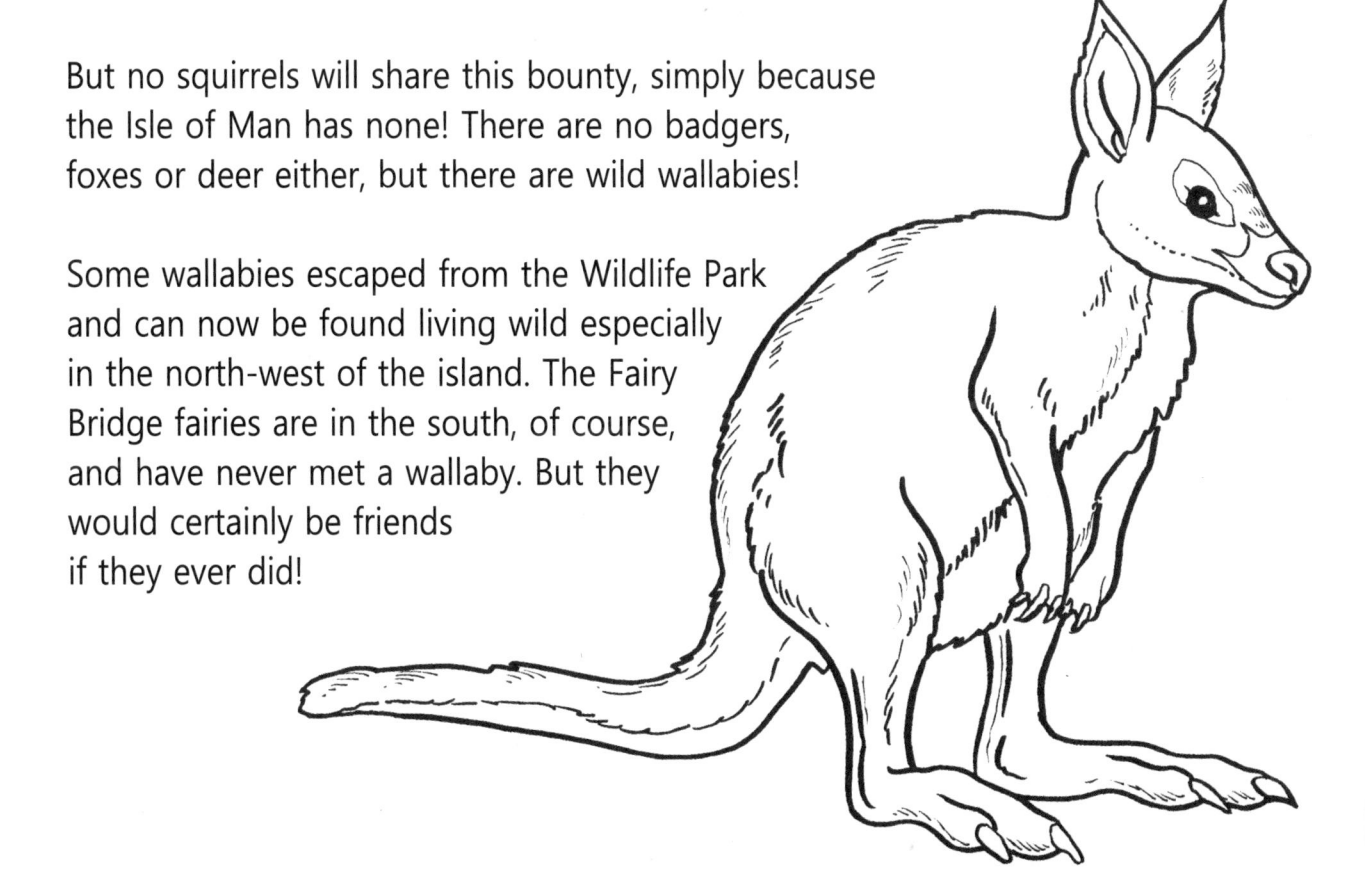

But no squirrels will share this bounty, simply because the Isle of Man has none! There are no badgers, foxes or deer either, but there are wild wallabies!

Some wallabies escaped from the Wildlife Park and can now be found living wild especially in the north-west of the island. The Fairy Bridge fairies are in the south, of course, and have never met a wallaby. But they would certainly be friends if they ever did!

With their still empty baskets, Iris and Marigold skip joyfully ahead of the others so they are the first fairies to meet the soft, brown rabbit. She towers above them, but this gentle creature doesn't frighten them. As Azalea and the three boys catch up with them, two sparrows also join the little gathering.

They all chat magically about the woods around the bridge. The birds cheep cheerfully and the fairies clap with delight upon hearing the rabbit's news about her kittens who love nothing better than scampering through the undergrowth, playing their own version of 'Chase'!

Their rabbit friend gives Marigold some of the soft fur which falls quite naturally from her tail. The fluffy tail fur makes the most comfortable pillows for the little fairy beds.

The sparrows fill Elder and Juniper's baskets with loose feathers before flying away. The fairies wrap themselves in feathers to keep them warm at night. The tail fur and the little feathers will be added to the fairies' bedding supplies when they return after their walk.

They will be kept clean and dry in an old tobacco tin on the fifth lowest brick jutting out under the south side of their bridge.

Their last interesting meeting is with a little, black spider. As always, the fairies magically swap news with their eight-legged pal. Then they continue on their way, thanking the spider for his gift of a beautifully symmetrical cobweb.

Iris carries this precious cargo in her basket and she will be certain to lift it carefully into a matchbox kept specially for cobwebs. You might be surprised to learn that the fairies use cobwebs instead of plasters. Yes, these delicate but slightly sticky threads can stem bleeding!

The contents of the matchbox are thankfully rarely needed, but can always be found on the sixth lowest brick jutting out under the south side of their bridge.

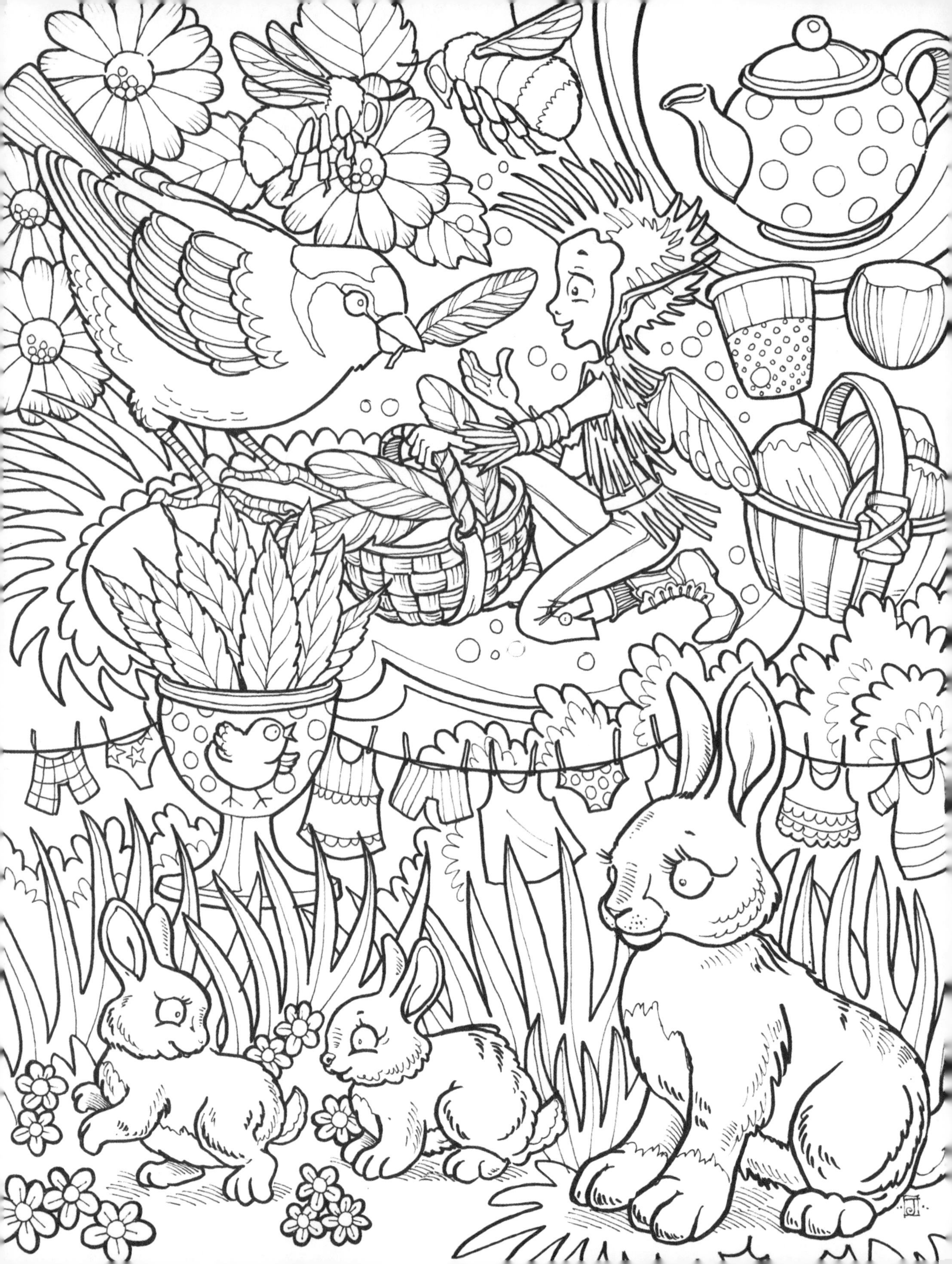

Chapter 5

While all these other events are happening, a large group of fairies sit on the grassy bank by the stream, sewing merrily in the sunshine.

There are lots of stories with elves making shoes and boots for shoemakers, but few people realise that fairies are excellent tailors and shoemakers too.

Oak and Linden are making trousers in all shades of green from the lightest lime to the green so dark it is almost black. Dahlia and Salvia are stitching satin tops for the girl fairies in soft blues, lilacs, creams, peaches, pale yellows and baby pinks.

Each boy fairy will later sew his own top from material magically patterned with his own needle or leaf. Almost all the girl fairies will produce their own beautiful skirts to match the petals of their flower, except for Flora and Fleur whose skirts are always patterned with lots of flowers.

Clematis and Thistle are occupied with knitting lacy, white ankle socks for all the girls. Their knitting needles are actually dried leaf stalks from an apple tree which have been shaped into a point at one end. They use white wool which was a gift from some friendly white sheep.

As each pair is finished, they fold the socks together and put them in the lid of an old jam jar. The socks will be stored on the lowest brick jutting out slightly under the north side of their bridge.

The boys' ankle socks are being knitted in a similar way but they are plainer than the girls'. Ginkgo and Hornbeam use brown wool donated by Loaghtan sheep. These Manx native sheep always amaze tourists as the rams grow four large, uniquely-shaped horns!

When finished, the boys' socks are also folded together then put in an old plastic pot which once had a flip-up lid with little mint sweets inside. Later, the pot will be placed proudly on the second lowest brick jutting out under the north side of their bridge.

A beautiful, blue butterfly flutters over her busy friends, knitting and sewing peacefully. She pauses by Fuchsia and Beech as if to inspect their needlework on the minute fairy undergarments. She seems to approve of their efforts and gives them a special double flap of her wings before flying off in search of flower nectar.

Yet more fairies are making pyjamas. These garments are for boys or girls – no-one really minds! Gorse, Lavender and Mimosa cut and stitch pyjama trousers out of plain cotton fabrics in all colours imaginable. Aspen, Poplar and Cypress cut and sew matching pyjama jackets, with the special slits in the backs for fairy wings – all fairy clothes have these slits, of course.

Fir and Heather fold the pairs of pyjamas together and place them tidily in a bright red, plastic lid which was previously on a spray can of furniture polish. Before lunch the red container will be put back in its usual place on the third lowest brick jutting out under the north side of their bridge.

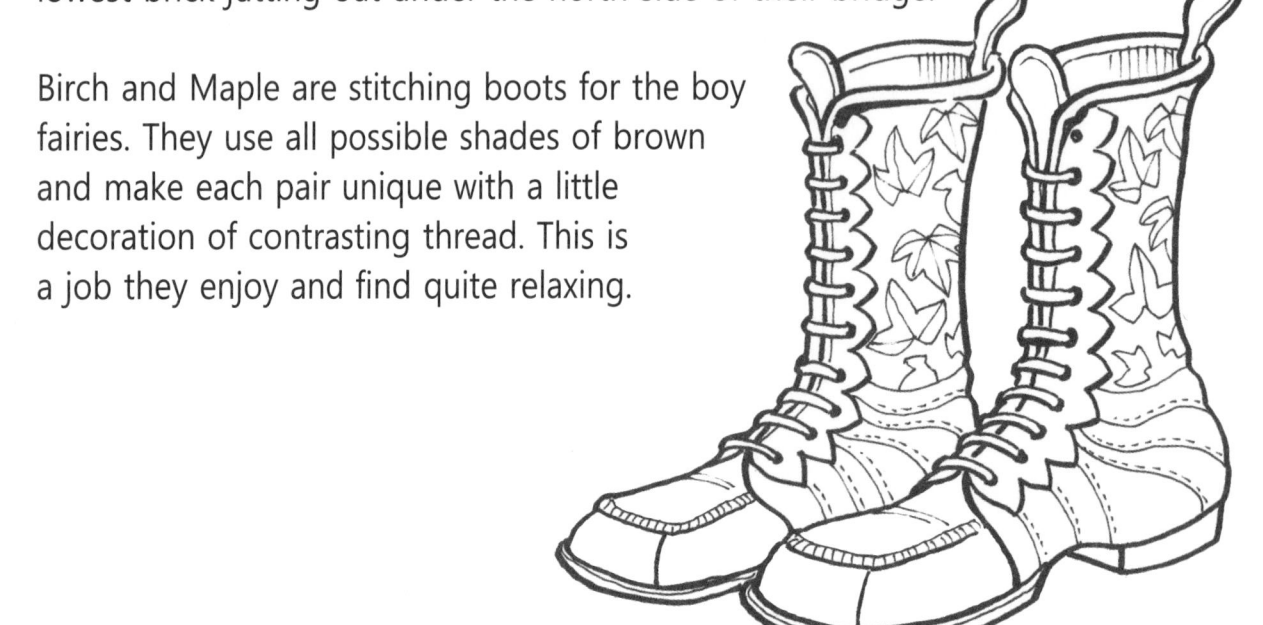

Birch and Maple are stitching boots for the boy fairies. They use all possible shades of brown and make each pair unique with a little decoration of contrasting thread. This is a job they enjoy and find quite relaxing.

Tulip and Honeysuckle agree with the boys and smile contentedly as they sew ballet-style pumps for their female friends. They choose material in the very same soft blues, lilacs, creams, peaches, pale yellows and baby pinks to match the fairy tops.

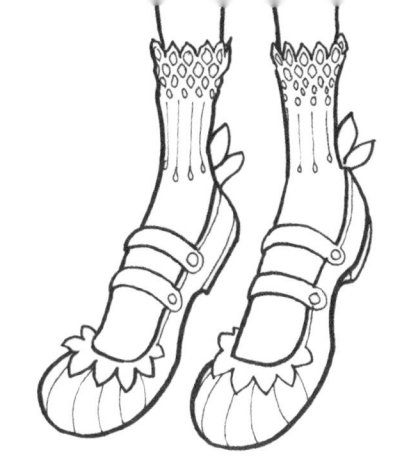

Each fairy will keep their own trousers or skirts, tops and shoes or boots in a neat pile next to where he or she sleeps on the higher bricks jutting out under both the north and south sides of their bridge.

You probably didn't know that fairies are proud beings and always take great care in their appearance. It is for this reason that all their clothes and footwear are the very best quality and always co-ordinate. A scruffy or bedraggled fairy is simply unheard of!

Chapter 6

It is now nearly lunchtime. Breakfast seems a long time ago and all the fairies are feeling rather hungry. Wonderful smells drift around the Fairy Bridge and everyone happily makes their way to the underside of the bridge.

Well, almost everybody. The six fairies on duty by the roadside above them will eat in a short while when they swap places with their six friends who will do the afternoon shift.

You don't need to worry about Bramble, the twins and the others because the guard duty is the fairies' favourite occupation. They all love taking turns on this job and are even on watch throughout the night. So it is always best to greet the Fairy Bridge fairies when you cross over their bridge. You will only have yourself to blame for the consequences if you don't!

So almost all the fairies are waiting patiently with their acorn cups in hand. One by one, Buttercup, Crocus and Acer serve them all with the delicious nettle soup they have been busily cooking this morning.

The saucepan is a white, enamelled tin cup with a line of royal blue running around its rim. It is one of the fairies' prized possessions although no-one is quite sure where it had come from. Perhaps it had been lost by a child on a camping trip long ago? The soup ladle is just a small twig with a natural hollow at one end.

After drinking the soup, Pine and Carnation dish up dessert: everyone gets a little leaf plate with a sprinkle of pumpkin and sunflower seeds served with a smear of honey. To the fairies, this is as tasty a treat as perhaps flapjack or cookies to you!

Conifer, Primrose and Laurel collect up the used acorn cups and wash them all in an oyster shell of water magically collected from the stream.

They arrange them on the grass in a patch of sunlight to dry, then set about washing their saucepan and ladle too. Obviously, the leaf plates need not be cleaned. Everything else will be collected up later, ready to use again.

The acorn cups and cooking equipment will be stored safely in an old margarine tub the fairies had found floating in the stream long ago. Of course, the tub was washed most carefully before its first use. It will soon be returned to its place on the fourth lowest brick jutting out under the north side of their bridge.

Fairies are natural beings and they live very happily amongst all the nature in the countryside. They find most of what they require around them, only ever taking as much as they actually need, re-using and recycling wherever possible.

margarine

As you know, they are great friends with all the living creatures around them, from tiny ants, to hedgehogs and even with animals much larger than themselves such as cats and dogs. In fact, if you are out for a walk with your dog and the two of you happen to meet a fairy, your pet will never bark at the miniature, magical being. In an unspoken agreement between all canines and fairies, dogs will never betray the presence of the fairy even to their beloved owners!

Chapter 7

After lunch and a little rest Poppy, Lobelia and Forsythia take the place of the twins and Bluebell on duty by the bridge above them.
They have only been on duty for a matter of seconds when a silver Isle of Man bus crosses the bridge on its journey north to Ramsey. The bus driver nods his greeting to the unseen fairies, which pleases all three of the girls.

An elderly lady passenger on the bus is fluent in Manx, so she is able to say, "Fastey mie, Mooinjer Veggey", which means, "Good afternoon, Fairies".
Just as before, the fairies cheer at her use of Manx. Everyone is wishing the lady a good afternoon too as Yew and Fern arrive to replace the boy fairies on duty. Hawthorn flies up to join them on the bridge's parapet a few moments later.

Immediately the boys spring into action when a blue tractor trundles past. The farmer gives a silent salute to the fairies and they salute happily back.

On the top deck of the bus, however, is quite a different situation. A father with a toddler on his lap says hello and his little girl copies him. But his nine year old son on the seat beside them says nothing at all.

"James, say hello to the fairies. Quick!" the dad says as the bus nears the bend in the road just after the bridge. But his stubborn son shakes his head.

"It's probably not too late yet James; we can still see the Fairy Bridge through the rear window," the dad implores. "Fairies are stupid!" the naughty boy exclaims loudly. The father shakes his head sadly as the bus continues on its way north.

Unseen by all the humans, the fairies are horrified. After a few seconds of stunned silence, the girl fairies hold hands and raise their arms up to the sky. Nothing at all seems to happen as they wordlessly drop hands, but the mischievous magic is done.

Later, as he gets off the bus, James will come to regret his harsh words. He will fall and twist his ankle, resulting in a nasty sprain.

When the doctor examines his bruised foot, she will tell James' parents that he must stay at home and rest for a whole week.

James will have to miss the Sunday School picnic, which he had been looking forward to. All his friends will have a marvellous time!

The next vehicle to pass the bridge is a taxi. It is carrying a couple of tourists who have just flown to the Isle of Man's airport. As the driver takes them north from Ronaldsway to the holiday cottage Mr and Mrs White have rented in Laxey, he starts telling them all about the island.

Approaching the Fairy Bridge, he tells them that it is customary to say hello to the fairies. The tourists laugh but Mr White joins the driver in wishing the fairies a good afternoon just as they cross the bridge.

"Superstitious nonsense!" exclaims Mrs White rudely.

The taxi driver is saddened by her words and attitude, but the fairies are disgusted. Just as before, the three girls hold hands and raise their arms up to the sky. Just as before, nothing at all seems to happen as they soundlessly drop hands, but again the mischievous magic is done.

Later that day, the Whites will start exploring Laxey. They will have a wonderful time visiting the famous Laxey Wheel then go to a little restaurant for their evening meal. Mr White will compliment his wife on her pretty, new dress. Unfortunately, Mrs White is going to spill her glass of red wine all over her dress. Red wine is difficult to wash out and Mrs White's pretty, new dress will be ruined!

Following behind the taxi is a rather battered, green car with an elderly man at the wheel. He is wearing quite tatty clothes with holes in his sleeves and an ancient flat cap over his grey hair.

To the relief and delight of the unseen fairies, the old man raises his cap to them as he drives over the bridge. The girls smile and bid him a good afternoon as he continues on his journey.

None of the fairies is at all bothered by the elderly gentleman's scruffy appearance or battered vehicle. Any type of polite greeting is all that matters to them!

A red Isle of Man Post Office van is next over the bridge. The driver waves a cheery hello to the fairies who approve and wave in return. Of course, the post woman doesn't see the tiny, magical folk as she carries on her way south west to deliver parcels in the old village of Port St Mary.

Her final delivery of the day is a most mysterious-looking parcel in a long tubular package. It's going to a quaint, thatch-roofed cottage in the hamlet of Cregneash which looks out over the Sound and the Calf of Man. The post woman never does discover what was in the strange parcel!

Luckily, all of the traffic for the rest of the afternoon will pass politely by with all manner of greetings. No more mischievous, fairy magic will be needed!

Chapter 8

But more fairy magic may be needed that afternoon, although it will not be the capricious kind.

While some fairies are resting before or after their turn on watch by the bridge, others are gathering ingredients and preparing the evening meal. But most of our little, fairy friends spend their time flying, reading and sprinkling fairy dust.

You see, there is a sycamore tree which grows by the stream. It is quite a tall tree and can easily be reached by humans standing on the Fairy Bridge itself. In fact, there is a little lay-by on the north side of the road at that exact spot so that cars can safely stop there if need be. But why do people want to stop there?

It isn't simply to visit the Fairy Bridge. The sad truth is that the actual bridge looks quite boring to human eyes. The fairies are too little for most of us to see them and all their stores are below the bridge, out of sight to anyone standing on the bridge. There are no handy steps and no path to get down to the bottom of the bridge. It simply wouldn't occur to visitors to even attempt it.

No, human visitors stay on the bridge by the sycamore tree. It turns out that the tree itself is important! The tree is old and over 10 metres tall. It has a strong trunk and the canopy of branches and leaves is quite high above any humans' heads.

Many visitors write wishes or little messages and tie them onto the tree trunk. Some people tie photos of their loved ones and some even tie on the Order of Service booklets from a funeral or wedding or baptism.

The fairies devote most afternoons to all of these. They fly up to them and magically read every single one, no matter what language the humans have used.

Wherever they can, the fairies flutter their wings and sprinkle a little fairy dust over the messages, hopes and so on.

The fairies love to help grant wishes.

Some wishes are within the scope of the fairy magic, so a little girl who wished for a puppy was granted her wish. And a little boy who wished for a birthday party had his wish come true too.

But the woman who wanted to sell her house and buy another one did not get her wish completely granted by the fairies. It was too big a wish for them, even though they all worked together on it.

However, with a wonderful sprinkle of magical fairy dust, the flowers in the lady's garden looked particularly beautiful on the day that a young couple called Mr and Mrs Strong came to look round her house.

"What a pretty garden,"
Mr Strong had said as he rang the doorbell.
"Yes," his wife had replied. "I've got a good feeling that we are going to like this Place."

And indeed they did fall in love with this house and so decided to buy it. Of course, the whole wish was too big for the fairies, but a lovely sprinkle of fairy dust certainly helped the wish to come true!

The woman selling the house is now living very happily in a little cottage in Peel, on the west coast of the island. She is particularly pleased with her view of the sea and the ancient, red sandstone castle. When she had signed the contracts of sale and her moving date had been arranged, she remembered the tiny fairies. She made another visit to the Fairy Bridge and threw some beautiful roses down by the stream for them. The fairies were delighted with this gift.

The fairies always appreciate any presents they receive. Many presents come to be their most prized possessions, such as the tiny teapot they were given long ago. It had actually been made for a child's doll house, but was the perfect size for the fairies. They are always most careful with the pretty, yellow teapot and keep it in pride of place on the highest brick jutting out under the north side of the bridge.

The fairies are very busy with sprinkling their magical, fairy dust over all the good memories and hopes and wishes of visitors to the Fairy Bridge. They hardly even notice the passage of time. But as the sun tracks west over the bridge, marvellous aromas come from the fairies' saucepan below. Everyone realises that they are hungry!

Happy Birthday

BIRTHDAY BOY

Isle of Man Post Office

Chapter 9

With the exception of those on guard duty who will eat afterwards, all the fairies head towards the base of the bridge, acorn cup in hand once more. Hazel, Ginkgo and Clematis have produced a dandelion curry, which everybody declares to be delicious. The fairies sit companionably together on the grass, enjoying their food and the sunshine. There is laughter and chatter as they eat contentedly.

Afterwards, Snowdrop, Linden and Salvia give out the lavender biscuits they have baked for dessert. Pansy and Hornbeam serve peppermint tea from the tiny, yellow teapot, using the delicate wings of a sycamore seed as a tea strainer. This herbal tea goes very well with the still-warm biscuits.

As the fairies on evening duty fly up to the top of the bridge, Aspen, Cypress and Fuchsia collect up the acorn cups and clean them in an oyster shell of water magically collected from the stream.

They leave them on the grass to dry in the sun, then wash up the saucepan and ladle too. It will all be collected up later and stored tidily in the margarine tub, ready to use again tomorrow.

Fir, Poplar and Oak decide to watch over the north side of the bridge. They are horrified when Lobelia tells them about naughty James and rude Mrs White. They wonder if they will need any mischievous magic this evening.

The afternoon guard fairies fly down for their curry as soon as Hyacinth, Tulip and Dahlia replace the boys on duty on the road going south. In no time at all, a motorcycle passes them. The rider tips his head towards the bridge and the girls give him a wave in return. But of course he doesn't see them as he heads home to Colby.

Other traffic crosses the bridge with everyone greeting the unseen fairies in one way or another. But then a large, black car drives by on its way north to the village of Maughold.
The passenger in the car wishes the fairies a good evening in Manx:
"Fastey mie, Mooinjer Veggey," ('good afternoon' and 'good evening' are the same in Manx).
The fairies clap and cheer, bidding her a good evening too. But the car driver says nothing.

Mrs Cowley turns to her husband, looking puzzled. "You didn't say hello to the fairies, Albert," she says.
"We don't have time for all that silliness," Mr Cowley states crossly.
"We're late enough as it is!"
"But it would only take a second as you drive along anyway," Mrs Cowley protests, but her obstinate husband refuses to listen.

The boys are appalled and no words are needed as they hold hands and raise their arms up to the sky. Just as before, nothing at all seems to happen. But as the boy fairies drop hands, the mischievous magic is done.

When he turns into his driveway later, Mr Cowley will still be rather bad tempered. He makes this turn most days without any problems at all. But not today. Today he is cross and in a rush. He won't look properly and will turn too quickly. There will be a loud, nasty sound as he hits the gatepost and the car scrapes right along one side.

Mr Cowley will jump angrily out of the car to inspect the damage. His wife will join him and look sadly at the long, jagged scratch in the car's shiny, black paintwork. It will run right along the car's front wing, along the driver's door and right up to the rear passenger door.

"Oh dear," she is going to say. "That is a terrible scratch but we can get it fixed," Mrs Cowley will add consolingly.
"It's my beautiful, new car," Mr Cowley will shout.
"It was perfect and I wanted it to stay perfect!"

Furiously, he is going to kick the gatepost, hurting his foot as he does so. Then Mr Cowley will have to hobble round to the passenger seat of the car, nursing his bruised toes. Shaking her head sadly at her foolish husband, but wisely saying nothing, Mrs Cowley will drive up to their house and park expertly by their front door.

Meantime, the six fairies on duty sit peacefully in the evening sunshine. Their friends below them are sewing, or sleeping, or chatting. One small group of fairies sing songs about magical times long ago. All is right with the fairy world!

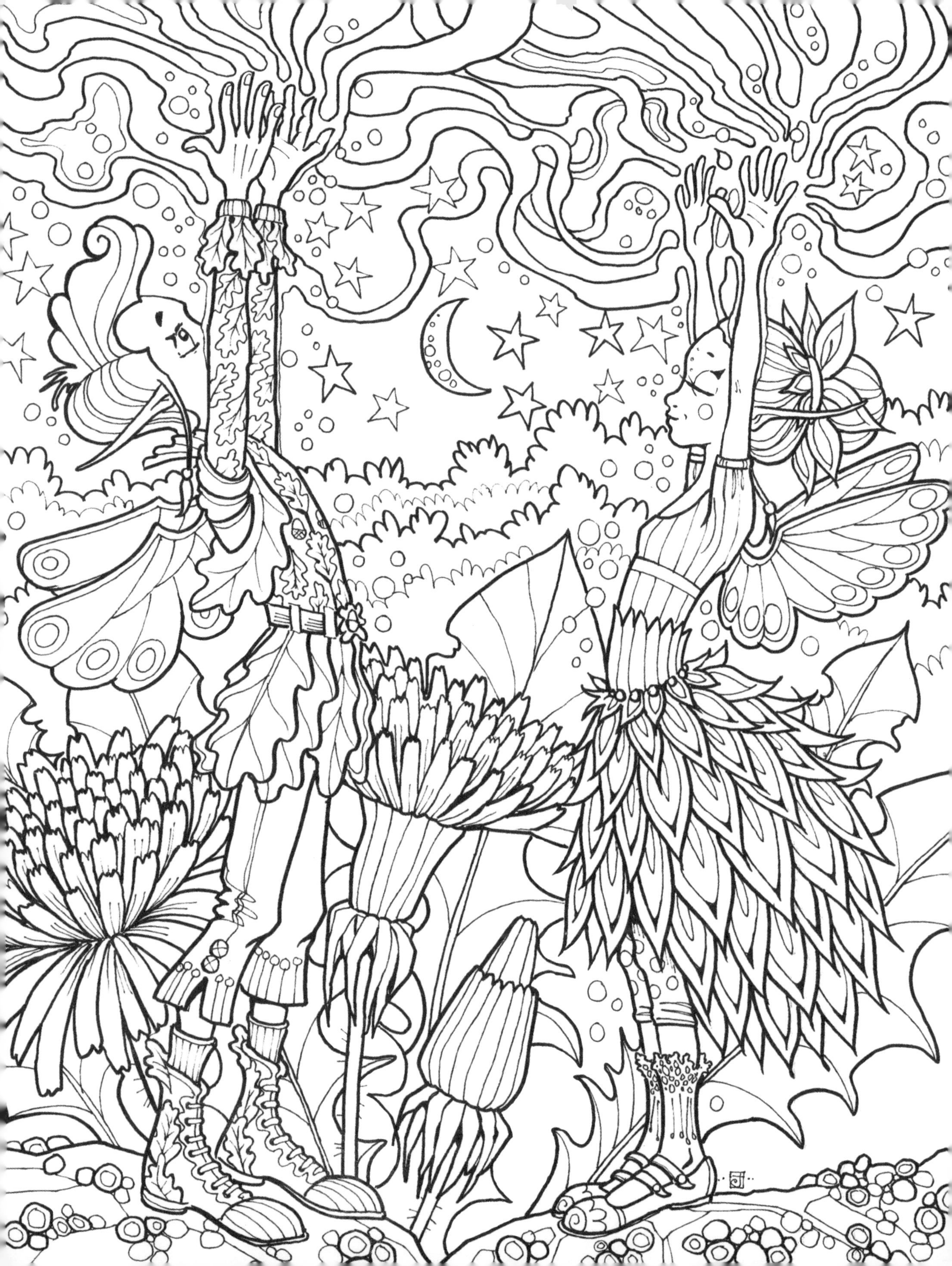

Chapter 10

As the evening draws to a close, the fairies begin preparing for bed. With faces washed and teeth brushed, they put on their pyjamas. Clothes that are to be worn again are folded neatly and placed next to each fairy's sleeping space with their footwear. Clothes for washing are collected in an old, plastic money bag that one of the fairies found snagged in a bush last winter.

Do you remember the six fairies who will be on guard on the bridge tonight? The ones who were foraging earlier and met the rabbit? Well, Azalea and the others take up their positions by the roadside, releasing their friends so they may also prepare for bed.

They will need no capricious magic at all tonight. The only event of note takes place soon after their duty starts. A lorry on its way to Port Erin crosses the bridge with a clanking sound as its contents rattle together in the back. The lorry driver blows a kiss to the fairies who are delighted.

Giggling, they blow kisses back and Juniper pretends to faint, falling backwards off the wall in a swoon! He flutters his wings and returns to his place, pretending to fan his face. His companions laugh and store this tale to tell the other fairies tomorrow.

It grows dark over the Isle of Man. Each fairy collects some fluffy, rabbit tail fur for a pillow and some soft feathers for blankets from the old tobacco tin. They snuggle down in their little, fairy beds on the various higher bricks jutting out under the bridge, wrapping themselves in cosily.

Good night, Fairy Bridge fairies!

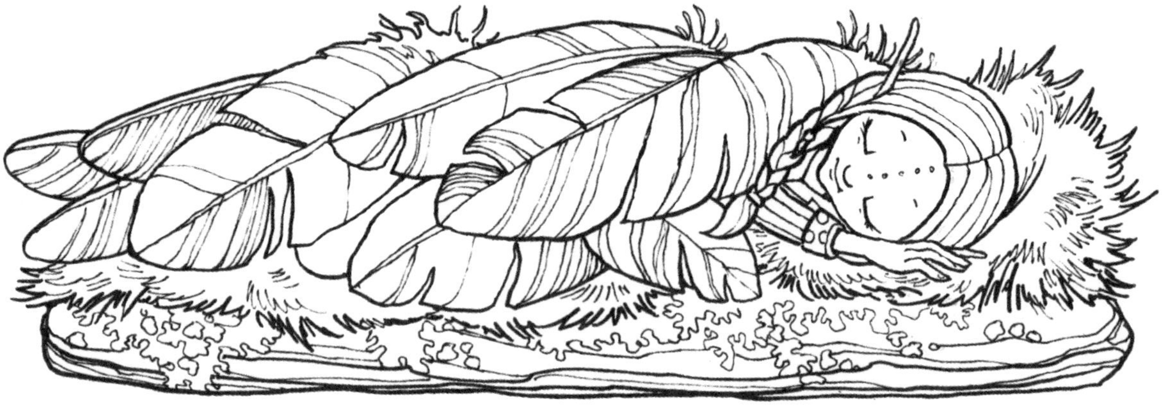

The Fairy Bridge Fairies

Girls (35)

Rose	Flora	Fleur	Crocus	Azalea
Violet	Daisy	Buttercup	Snowdrop	Clematis
Daffodil	Tulip	Honeysuckle	Salvia	Thistle
Fuchsia	Freesia	Heather	Bluebell	Mimosa
Hyacinth	Pansy	Carnation	Dahlia	Lavender
Iris	Lily	Marigold	Lilac	Gorse
Poppy	Lobelia	Forsythia	Primrose	Buddleia

Boys (35)

Bramble	Oak	Birch	Spruce	Juniper
Cedar	Maple	Chestnut	Alder	Elder
Acer	Hickory	Ash	Hornbeam	Rowan
Willow	Linden	Yew	Sycamore	Laurel
Fern	Ivy	Hazel	Hawthorn	Mistletoe
Elm	Holly	Cypress	Poplar	Ginkgo
Beech	Pine	Fir	Conifer	Aspen

Manx Notes (with 'how to say it' guide)

Fairies – Mooinjer Veggey (Moindga Vega – to rhyme with 'beggar')

Good morning – Moghrey mie (Morra my)

Good afternoon/evening – Fastey mie (Fasta – to rhyme with 'Pasta' – my)

* 'Mooinjer Veggey' literally means 'People Little' – describing words come after the noun in Manx. So 'Moghrey mie' = 'Morning good' and so on.

** The 'how to say it' advice in brackets above is only for guidance!

Draw your own fairies

Further Isle of Man stories:
The Really Wild Wildlife Park
Daisy's Days Out
Wallababies

The Buttons Collection
1. Hello Buttons!
2. Buttons in Trouble!
3. Buttons on Holiday
4. Christmas Buttons
5. Buttons Has a Plan
6. Easter Buttons
7. Buttons and the TT
8. Buttons in Love!
9. Buttons Visits the Vet
10. Buttons Saves the Day